W9-AGD-647

What is ecology?

Every living thing that is known to exist is found on one planet, the Earth. They all share this planet, from bacteria too small to be seen without a microscope to the giant redwood trees and the whales of the oceans.

All the living and non-living things that surround such a plant or animal are called its environment. For example, the environment of a plant includes the soil, the water and foodstuffs in the soil and the air the plant is growing in. Rainfall and temperature may affect the life of the plant as well as other plants which may compete for water and food. There could also be animals which eat the plant and some which may help it to reproduce. All these things make up the plant's environment. The science that looks at the ways in which plants and animals affect their environment and are affected by it is called 'ecology'.

WATER ECOLOGY

Jennifer Cochrane

Series Consultant: John Williams, C.Biol.,M.I.Biol.
Series Illustrator: Cecilia Fitzsimons, B.Sc.,Ph.D.

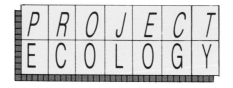

Air Ecology
Animal Ecology
Land Ecology
Plant Ecology
Urban Ecology
Water Ecology

First published in 1987 by
Wayland (Publishers) Ltd
61 Western Road, Hove
East Sussex BN3 1JD, England

British Library Cataloguing in Publication Data

Cochrane, Jennifer
    Water ecology. — (Project ecology)
    1. Aquatic ecology — Juvenile literature
    I. Title   II. Series
    574.5'263 QH541.5.W3

    ISBN 0–85078–892–7

Typeset in the UK by
DP Press Ltd, Sevenoaks, Kent
Printed in Italy by
G. Canale & C.S.p.A., Turin
Bound in Belgium by
Casterman S.A.

Series Editor: Philip Parker

Jennifer Cochrane studied Freshwater Biology at Leicester University and was a teacher before joining Macdonald & Co. Publishers. She was Editor-in-Chief of Macdonald's Junior Reference Library and is the author of many titles on ecology and the natural world.

John Williams is a former head teacher and a school science advisor. He is Honorary Secretary of the School Natural Science Society.

Cecilia Fitzsimons is a science-trained artist who specializes in natural history and biological illustrations. She has a doctorate in marine cell biology and has taught science.

Cover: bottom *killer whale exhaling through its blow hole,* left *freshwater green algae,* right *the Victoria Falls on the border between Zambia and Zimbabwe.*

Frontispiece: *the Earth from space showing Africa and Antarctica.*

Contents

1. The water planet

An alien, arriving on Earth from space, would probably expect to communicate with living things in the seas. About 70 per cent of the surface of the planet is under water while the land is covered by clouds made up of water droplets.

Scientists are unsure as to where the water originally came from. It was probably released as clouds of steam from newly formed rocks as the Earth was cooling. When the Earth's surface became cool enough, the vapour turned into liquid and fell to form the first oceans some 4,000 million years ago. Volcanoes may also have been responsible for much of the water since they release water as vapour and liquid from inside the Earth.

Water can exist as either a solid, a liquid or a vapour (gas). Below temperatures of 0°C it is ice. Above 100°C it all becomes a vapour. Between these temperatures it exists as a liquid and remains a liquid for the temperatures most suited to life on Earth.

Life on Earth began in the oceans and a special quality of water would have played an important role. Water is able to dissolve more

The volcanic island of Surtsey, which emerged from the sea bed in 1963. It is likely that most of the Earth's water was released as steam from newly formed rocks as the Earth was cooling. Water vapour is still released into the air by volcanoes.

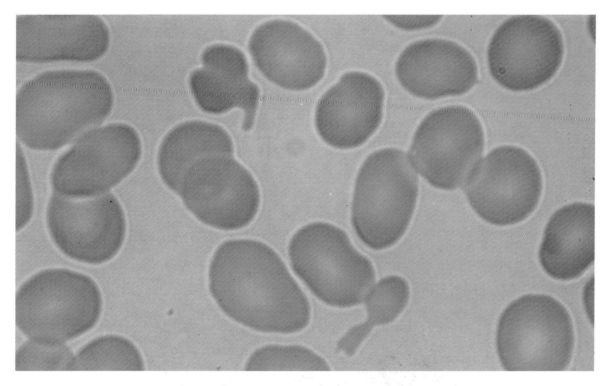

substances than any other liquid. So the early seas would have contained a great deal of materials from which the first basic 'building blocks' of life could have formed. The earliest plants and animals lived in water and it was many millions of years before some kinds adapted to live on dry land. Yet life in water has an advantage over life on land since it is less likely to 'dry up'.

Water is a vital part of every living thing. You may think you are quite solid but about 60 per cent of the human body is made up of water. Indeed, most animals and plants are about half water.

The bodies of living things are made up of tiny cells. Humans, for instance, each contain some 1,000 billion cells and each cell contains water. Blood in animals and sap in plants are mostly water, and carry dissolved gases and food to make life possible. In many living things, the water keeps the cells rigid so

A close-up view of human blood cells. Blood is mostly made up of water.

that they may hold their shape. For instance, a plant left in the Sun will wilt due to water loss.

Water is also necessary for the process called photosynthesis, where green plants use the energy of the Sun to convert water and carbon dioxide into food and oxygen. All other living things on the planet are dependent on green plants as a source of food and the oxygen is essential for most animals to breathe.

Sunlight penetrates to a depth of about 100m in the seas and it is in this layer that the tiny floating plants called phytoplankton are found. These plants take in the dissolved chemicals in the seas and photosynthesize, making the basic food supply for the animal life in the oceans and giving out the greatest part of the oxygen that is released into the air.

2. Where is all the water?

The Earth's water is spread right through the planet. It is easy to see where most of the liquid water is by looking at a map of the world. It is in the oceans and seas, and in the rivers and lakes. The oceans and seas contain water that has much dissolved salt in it. Water that contains little salt is called fresh water and is found in the rivers and lakes. Only 3 per cent of the planet's water is fresh water but it is a vital part since all the land-living animals and plants need it to survive.

Three-quarters of all the fresh water is locked up in another store. These are the ice caps at the poles. Water moves between these ice caps and the oceans. During the ice ages the ice caps grow much bigger and the sea level drops. If the temperature of the planet were to rise and the ice caps melt, the sea level would increase by about 100m and flood the lower levels of land.

Compared to the vast stores at the poles and in the seas, the air contains very little water. Yet without this amount there would be no weather like rain or snow. Some of the rain that falls drains into rivers and lakes, but much soaks into the soil and rocks.

The level at which water collects in the ground is called the water table. The water may be held in the spaces between the tiny soil particles, held in cracks in the rocks or absorbed by 'aquifers'. These are rocks like sandstone which can soak up a lot of water, rather like a sponge. This water will reappear as a spring where the water table meets the land surface on a hillside, and will run into a river or lake.

So, there is water throughout the planet. It is found inside living things as well as in the air, the ground and the seas.

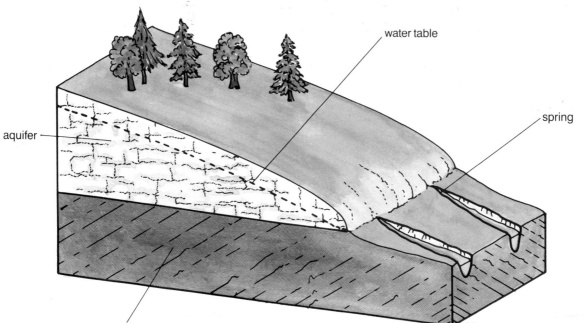

A cross-section through the land to show an aquifer.

Activity: Water in the soil

Plug the ends of the tubes with a small piece of filter paper and add the same height of sand to one, garden soil to another and clay to the third.

Place the ends of the tubes in a water bath and support them upright with the clamps. Make sure that you know which tube contains which soil and leave them for a few days.

After this time examine the levels of water soaked by the solids. Are they at different levels? How can you explain what you see? Which solid has the highest water level and which the lowest? What is the difference between these solids? If you were a farmer and wanted to grow crops, what type of land would you use, and why?

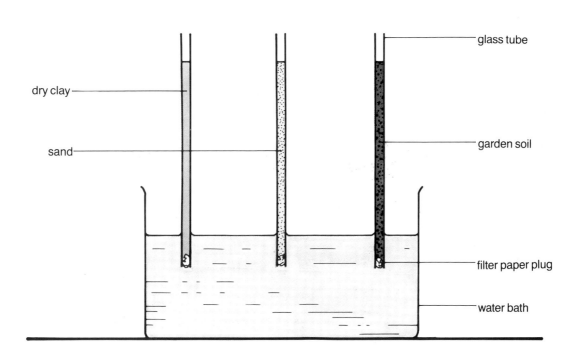

What this shows

Water is taken in by soil types and sand. Those substances that are made up of many fine solids take up more water than those composed of coarser, larger material. Liquids naturally rise through the tiny spaces between solids like soil, sand and clay and this process is called capillarity.

3. Water and warmth

The Moon is about the same distance from the Sun as the Earth. It is very hot on the side that points towards the Sun and −250°C on the other side. The Earth would be the same if it were not for the seas and gases of the atmosphere absorbing and storing the heat, and keeping the planet's temperature balanced enough for life.

Land absorbs and loses heat quickly but the vast oceans act like an enormous heat-controlling engine, absorbing and losing heat more slowly and carrying heat around the globe in the great ocean currents.

The surface of the seas and oceans is warmed by the Sun and since warm water is lighter than cold, a layer of warm water develops near to the surface. The winds will blow this top layer in a particular direction and colder water will rise to take its place, to be warmed in turn.

The moving water becomes a surface current and crosses the oceans. When it reaches a coast it warms the land. For instance, northern Europe is warmed by the Gulf Stream, which crosses the Atlantic Ocean from the Gulf of Mexico. This affects the climate. London is further north than New York, but its winters are not as severe.

The seas do not always warm the land. In places where the cold currents well up from the deep waters to replace the removed warm water, the effect is cooling. These cold currents also carry with them mineral salts from the depths and there are always more phytoplankton where they rise, providing food for the sea-living creatures.

The pattern of the many surface currents that cross the seas and oceans.

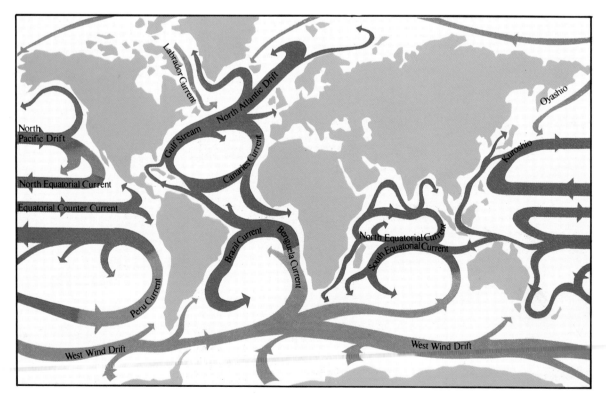

Activity: Warm water rises

What you will need

A tall heat-proof beaker full of water, a tripod, a heat source like a bunsen burner, a heat-proof gauze mat and some crystals of potassium permanganate.

What this shows

When water is warmed it becomes less dense than cool water and it rises. In the experiment, this water cooled after rising and so it fell down towards the bottom of the beaker. This results in the movement of currents of warm water and such movements are called 'convection' currents.

Put the beaker of warm water on the tripod and drop in a crystal of potassium permanganate. Gently heat the bottom of the beaker with the burner and watch what happens.

The crystal gives out a purple colour as it dissolves and streamers of this colour rise up the beaker. Why does this happen? These streamers will also fall after rising. What is the reason for this?

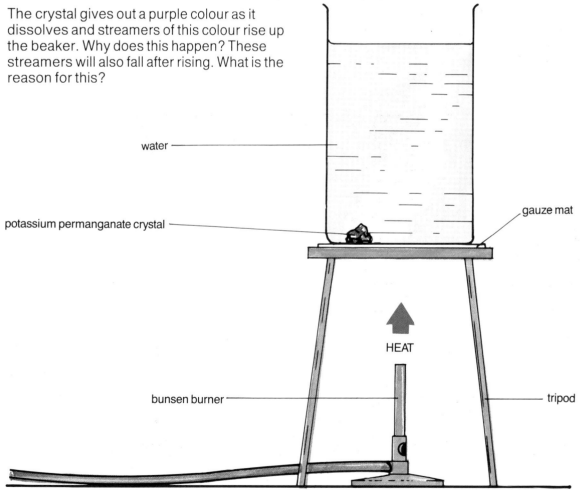

water

potassium permanganate crystal

gauze mat

HEAT

bunsen burner

tripod

4. Water the solvent

One of the most important things about water is that it is a very good solvent. This means that it is good at dissolving things. If you taste sea water, you taste the many mineral salts that are dissolved in the sea. As water runs over the soil and the rocks on its way to the sea, it dissolves part of them.

Even though only tiny amounts of salts are dissolved, usually too small to be tasted in stream or river water, they have built up in the seas. This is because the water carrying the mineral salts evaporates from the seas, leaving the salts behind. As more and more water flows into the sea and then evaporates, the sea water becomes saltier. There are salts of all the minerals on the planet dissolved in the sea. If enough sea water was used, it would be possible to recover even gold.

The cells in living things would not work if water was not such a good solvent. All the chemicals in each cell can react together because they are dissolved in water and free to move about. For example, oxygen dissolves in the blood of animals and can travel to food stores in the body to release energy. The resulting waste substances can also be removed so that they do not build up inside the cells and poison them.

It is because there are salts dissolved in the seas that the phytoplankton can make food. Although carbon dioxide and water are the main ingredients of the food made by plants, they are not the only ones. Plants need other elements like nitrogen and potassium to build up food substances and these are taken in with their water supply.

Unfortunately, water dissolves polluting substances just as easily as it dissolves the essential materials. Wastes from factories and chemicals like pesticides, sprayed on crops to kill insects, may end up in rivers and seas, affecting the plants and animals living there.

Salt can be removed from water by simply allowing it to evaporate in 'pans' as here in the Niger, in Africa.

Activity: A closer look at water

What you will need

A beaker filled with a little water, a tripod, a bunsen burner, a heat-proof gauze mat and some watch glasses (small heat-proof glass dishes) large enough to sit on the beakers. You will need water samples from various sources such as a tap, rain, pond or stream and distilled water. The use of a microscope would be an advantage.

Put a little of the water sample in the watch glass and place it on the beaker. Heat the water using the burner so that it boils. What happens to the water in the watch glass? When all the water has evaporated is there anything left? Any solid that remains is called the residue.

Remove the bunsen burner and wait for the watch glass to cool. Put this on one side and repeat the experiment with a sample from a different source. What do you find this time? Is there a residue?

If you have a microscope, place some of each residue on to clean microscope slides. Look at each residue through the microscope and compare your results.

What this shows

Water from different places contains varying amounts of dissolved substances. Even tap water is not pure, and leaves a residue of crystals of salt. Rainwater should not leave a residue. If there is a small amount, where do you think it came from (remembering how the water was collected)?

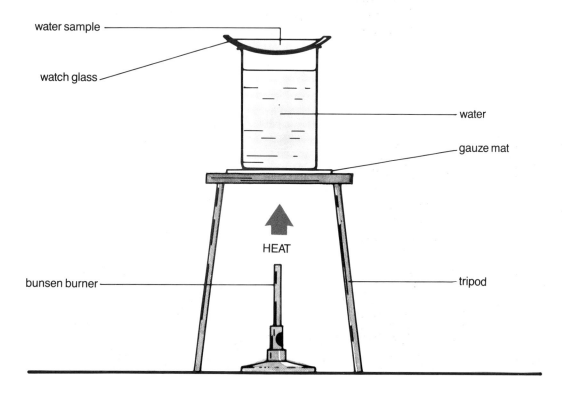

water sample

watch glass

water

gauze mat

HEAT

bunsen burner

tripod

5. The water cycle

Water, like most of the Earth's resources, is not only used once. It is used again and again, circling from the seas to the air, back to the ground through plants and animals and eventually back to the seas. It travels across the oceans in currents, through the air as vapour or in clouds and crosses the land as streams or rivers.

It may spend a long time locked up in the frozen ice caps or in the snow at the tops of mountains, but even this will eventually melt and liquid water will return to the seas. This movement of water is called the water cycle. If we follow the path of a droplet of water on such a journey we will see how the water cycle works.

The movement of water from the oceans to the atmosphere and back again is known as the water cycle.

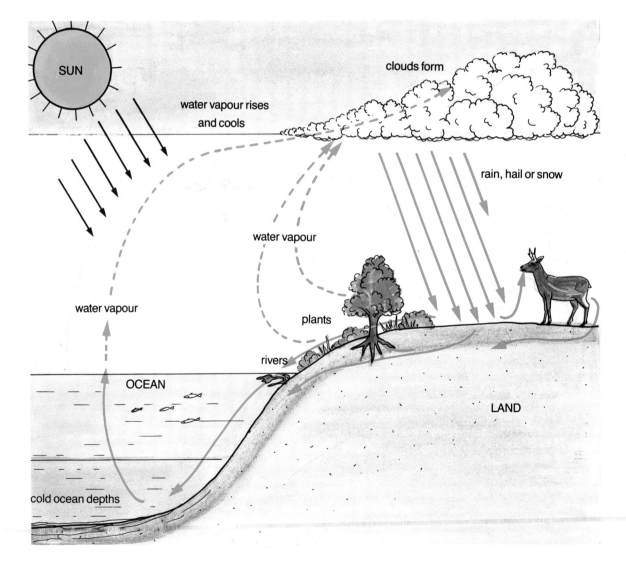

Fresh water may spend a long time trapped as ice. This iceberg is floating off the coast of Newfoundland.

The oceans and seas are the great reservoirs of the world. A droplet of water in the cold, dark depths of the ocean may be caught in a rising current and travel to the surface. It may then be warmed by the Sun and turn into a vapour, carried by the wind across the sea and over land.

If the air cools enough, the vapour will turn back to a liquid and may combine with more water to fall as rain, hail or snow.

The rainwater will drain into the soil or run off into rivers and lakes and may turn back to vapour if it is warm enough. It may be taken in by the roots of a plant and will soon evaporate from the leaves or it may be drunk by an animal and pass out as waste. If it remains a liquid it will journey to the sea in a river to start the cycle all over again.

The Niagara River connects Lake Erie and Lake Ontario in Canada.

6. Rain from the air

When air is warmed it rises and cools. The cooling may be enough to cause the water vapour in the air to turn into liquid droplets and form clouds, from which rain may fall.

There are two basic types of clouds. Sometimes the sky is covered by a large grey sheet and this is stratus cloud. These are formed by the gentle rising of large areas of air. Very low stratus cloud is called fog. Cumulus clouds stretch up high into the sky, sometimes so high that their water droplets turn to ice. These ice particles are caught in rising currents of air and as they travel upwards they collect an extra layer of ice, gain in weight and fall, only to be caught by another rising current. This may happen many times until they are so heavy that they fall to the ground as hail.

In these ways fresh water, on which all land-living plants and animals depend, returns to the planet from which it came. This water is not always pure, however. Dust and smoke particles may be washed out of the air and rainwater may be affected by pollution, giving rise to acid rain.

All rain is, in fact, slightly acid because it contains a weak acid formed from the carbon dioxide in the air. This is a good thing since it helps to dissolve minerals in the soil so they can be taken in more easily by plants.

Some gases given out by power stations, industries and vehicle exhausts will have a stronger effect. Gases like the oxides of nitrogen and sulphur will combine with the moisture in the air to give stronger acids which return to the land as acid rain, mist or snow. The acid water will drain into rivers and lakes, affecting the life there, and will be absorbed by the soil where it can affect the growth of plants.

In many parts of the world the seasonal monsoon rains are a vital source of water. This is Nepal during the monsoon rains.

Activity: Testing for acid rain

What you will need

A large plastic bottle, a polythene bag, rubber bands, and a wooden stake about 1.5 m long. You will also need some universal indicator solution, or papers, and the colour chart that is supplied with it.

Cut the top off the bottle so that you have a tall, beaker-shaped container. Use the polythene bag as a lining for the collector and secure it with rubber bands. Fix the collector to the wooden stake and place the stake in the ground away from any overhanging trees or buildings.

When it rains, note the direction of the clouds. Pour the collected rainwater into a clean, dry beaker and add a little of the indicator solution. Compare the colour with those on the chart and record the number that is indicated. This is a measure of how acid the water is. Repeat this for rain that is collected on different days with different wind directions. Compare the colour obtained with the result of adding the indicator solution to lemon juice, to milk and to distilled water.

The scale used to measure the acidity of a liquid is called the pH scale. Normal rainwater naturally has a pH of 5.6 and any number obtained under this scale will mean that the water is too acidic. Where may this have come from, remembering the wind direction? Lemon juice has a pH of 2 and so is much more acid. Milk has a pH of 6.5 and is a very weak acid. Pure water is neither acid nor alkali. It is neutral with a pH of 7.

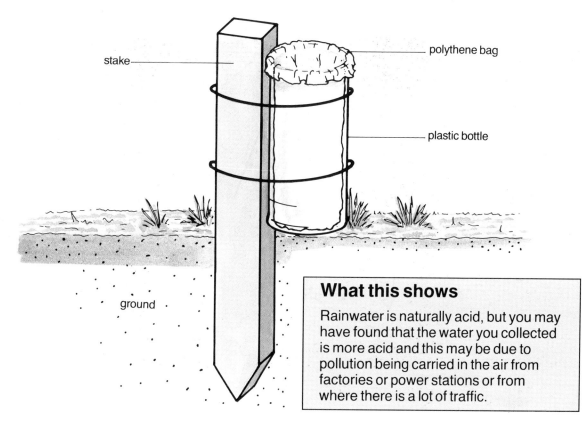

stake — polythene bag — plastic bottle — ground

What this shows

Rainwater is naturally acid, but you may have found that the water you collected is more acid and this may be due to pollution being carried in the air from factories or power stations or from where there is a lot of traffic.

7. Running waters

Rain or snow falls into what is called a 'catchment' area. This is an area of land that provides a river with its water. The water will trickle through the soil and rocks, dissolving minerals as it goes, and collect to form a stream, a spring or a pond. The stream or spring will lead into a river and so down to the sea.

The rainwater will not only pick up salts as it trickles through the catchment area. It will also collect fertilizers and pesticides from agricultural land. It may also trickle through places where poisonous chemicals have been buried, dissolve them and take them into the stream or lake.

Once in the stream, the water runs downwards. At the start it is called the headstream. Here the water is cool and runs fast. It has plenty of oxygen and carbon dioxide dissolved in it, collected as it drops over waterfalls and bubbles over stony shallows. It may carry pebbles and gravel along with it, helping to wear away the bed of the stream.

As the river gets further from its source it slows down and drops some of the gravel and stones that were being carried. Mud will also drop to the bottom, and rooted plants may grow here.

As the river leaves the hills and approaches the sea it changes. The lowland river is a much slower stretch of water, winding through flatter lands and there are often marshes alongside it. There is much less air dissolved in the water and it is more easily polluted. The final stretch of water is the estuary. This is where the seawater mixes with the fresh water, making the fine mud stick together and drop to the bottom, or be swept into the sea.

The edge of the Krug River in Tasmania. This river has been very badly polluted by copper mining.

Activity: Air in water

What you will need

A heat-proof flask with a bung fitted with a delivery tube, a water tank, a bunsen burner, a heat-proof gauze mat and a tripod, a collecting jar with a lid and a beehive shelf to stand it on. You will need water from a stream, a pond and a tap.

Set up the apparatus as shown, filling the flask, tube and tank with water. You will need to fill the collecting jar with water, put its lid over the top and turn it upside down, removing the lid when it is underwater.

Heat the flask with the burner. What do you notice? How much air can you 'recover'. Stop heating when no more bubbles appear.

Repeat the experiment with tap water and water from a pond.

What this shows

Water contains air dissolved in it. The water from a river will contain more air than water that has been still.

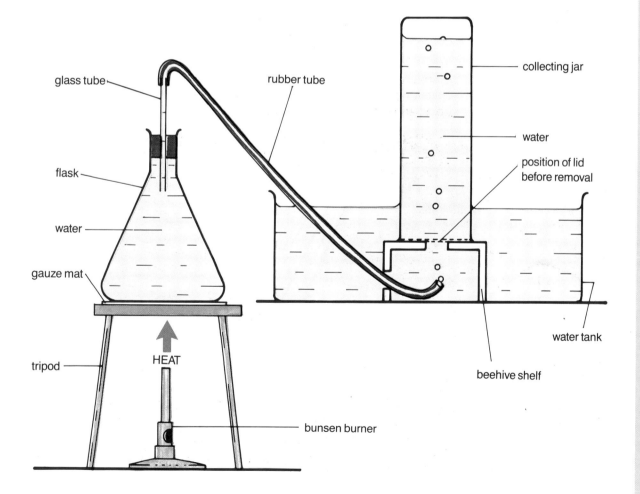

glass tube

rubber tube

collecting jar

water

position of lid before removal

flask

water

gauze mat

tripod

HEAT

bunsen burner

water tank

beehive shelf

8. Life in running water

With a strong current sweeping in one direction all the time, river plants must be anchored and animals must be good swimmers so they may stay in one place.

Few plants and animals live in the fast headstream waters. Flowering plants cannot take root until there is mud or gravel on the bed. Only algae, mosses and liverworts, which can fasten themselves to bare rock, can grow here. Insect larvae with strong claws to anchor themselves and strong-swimming fishes are also found here.

As the waters slow down, so that flowering plants can root themselves in the mud and gravel, there are more places to shelter animal life. Snails and worms, with insects and their larvae, live in and around the plants, with fishes eating them. Plankton is not found in running water. It drifts, and so would be swept away by the current.

Feeding on water plants and small animal life in rivers are roach. These fishes prefer to swim about in shoals.

These mayfly larvae have flattened bodies to offer the least resistance to running water and they have claws to anchor themselves to rocks. They need a lot of oxygen and are found only in unpolluted stretches of water.

In these slower waters, which have less air dissolved in them, pollution is more likely to occur. In normal conditions dead plants and animals are decayed with the help of insect larvae and worms, and then by bacteria. These all need oxygen to work. If something happens to reduce the amount of dissolved oxygen, then other bacteria that do not need air, the anaerobic bacteria, take over. They produce unpleasant smelling gases, such as methane and hydrogen sulphide, but they do decay the wastes.

This is how the wastes in water are naturally removed. If too much waste is put into a river, or if it is poisoned so that the bacteria cannot work, it will die. No living things will then be found in it.

Waiting for a fish to swim within grasping distance, a white egret stands still at the bank of a river in New South Wales, Australia.

9. Still waters

Still waters have plankton in them, since there is no current to wash them away. The food chains begin with the phytoplankton. These trap the Sun's energy and make food with water, carbon dioxide and mineral salts, producing oxygen. They can continue to make food while they have a good supply of salts but in still waters the salts can run out.

This problem does not usually arise in shallow ponds. The sunlight reaches right down into the water, and phytoplankton can photosynthesize, with plenty of salts dissolving out of the mud on the bottom.

However, in deeper ponds and lakes, there may be a problem. The Sun warms the top layer of the water, which then floats on the cool, deeper water. The warm water currents do not mix with the colder layer and they get warmer still, until the two layers are divided by a temperature difference, called a thermocline. Above the thermocline the top layer is warm and sunlit. The phytoplankton flourishes, and uses up all the salts. This layer is separated from the mud at the bottom by the layer of cold water, and food production will stop if there is a shortage of salts.

The cold, lower layer is darker and cooler. There are plenty of salts, but less sunlight. The plants produce a little oxygen, but the animals will use that up fairly quickly. Food production slows down through lack of light. If the phytoplankton in the upper layer grow very fast, they can cut out all the light in the lower depths and stop the food production.

Ponds and lakes stay like this until the autumn and spring. This is when the heating effect of the Sun changes and the waters are affected by gales allowing the levels to mix and nutrients to circulate.

Water-lilies are anchored to the bottom of the pond or lake by roots. They provide shelter and shade for the pond animals in hot weather.

Activity: Make a thermocline

What you will need

A water tank, two thermometers and warm and very cold water.

Pour some cold water into the tank and place the end of one of the thermometers in it. Hold the thermometer in place and wait for the reading to become constant. Record the temperature. Very gently pour the warm water onto the cold and hold the second thermometer in place in this water as shown. Record both temperatures every ten seconds. What do you see? Why don't the layers mix very much?

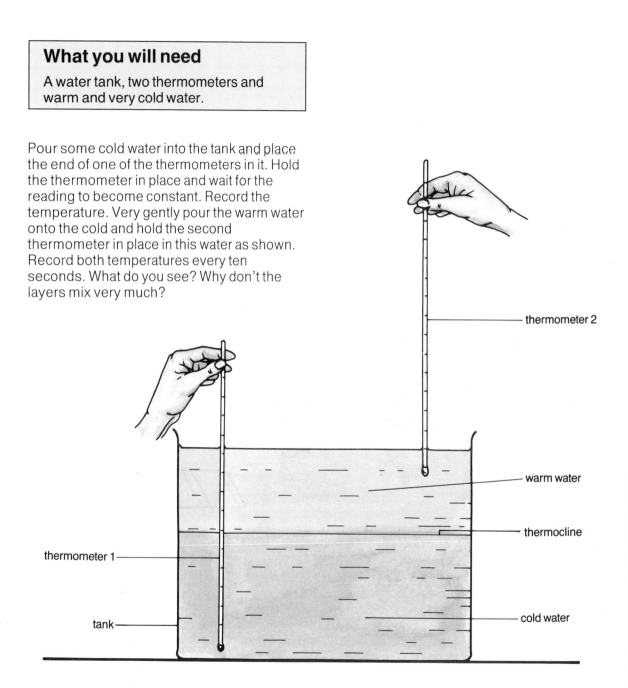

thermometer 2

warm water

thermocline

thermometer 1

cold water

tank

What this shows

If you were careful you would have made your own thermocline. The warm water will sit on top of the cold since it is lighter and the two layers will hardly mix.

10. Life in still waters

In warm, sunlit waters containing plenty of mineral salts the plankton can multiply until the waters are thick with them, providing plenty of food for the swimming animals. Freshwater animals include fishes, frogs, terrapins and water snakes, shrews, beavers and water voles, among others. The fishes feed directly on the plankton, filtering it out of the water passing through their gills.

There is a great variety of still water life, and the population of one pond may be completely different from another nearby.

Although many lakes have streams draining both into and out of them, there is no strong current sweeping away anything that is not anchored. Most of the flowering plants are rooted in the bottom mud, but some are free floating, their roots trailing in the water.

Mud collects on the bottom of still waters, made from the soil that washes into the water and the dead remains of plants and animals. The decaying remains are called detritus. The animals, like worms, are part of the decaying process that returns the elements to the water. Pollution begins when there is too much waste for them to digest, and the wastes poison the water, using up all the oxygen.

The mud provides salts for the pond and it also provides shelter for the animals when the weather gets too cold or too hot. When ice forms in the ponds, some fishes sink to the bottom and hibernate in the mud. If the heat dries up a pond, some fishes sink into the mud and make a cocoon of slime. They stay there until the water returns.

A food chain in still water. The plants and animals are not all shown to scale.

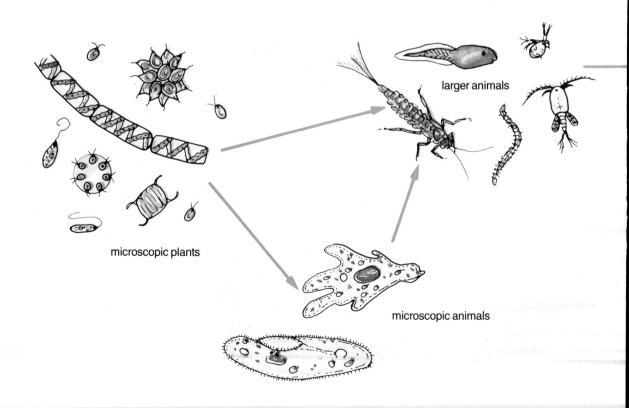

larger animals

microscopic plants

microscopic animals

Activity: Pond dipping

What you will need

A hand lens, some white plastic trays and a pond net. The net must have a fine mesh and can be made from the lower half of an old nylon stocking or a fine net curtain material stitched to a piece of curved wire and fixed to a long cane or pole.

Go to your local pond and watch the surface carefully. You may see insects on the surface or around plants on the water's edge.

Sweep the pond net quickly just under the surface of the water and lift it up. Try not to splash the water. Tip the contents of the net carefully into a tray which should have a little pond water in it. Do a few more sweeps with the net in the same place, each time emptying the contents into the tray.

Watch the tray carefully. After a while you may see some movement. Use the hand lens to examine the life and record the different types of creatures you find.

Always carry out your work at the waterside and return the creatures to the pond as soon as possible.

Sweep with your net in different places, towards the bank where it is shallow, for instance, and further out where it is deep. Also, sweep at different depths including along the bottom of the pond.

What this shows

The variety of pond life is easy to see and different creatures will be found in different places.

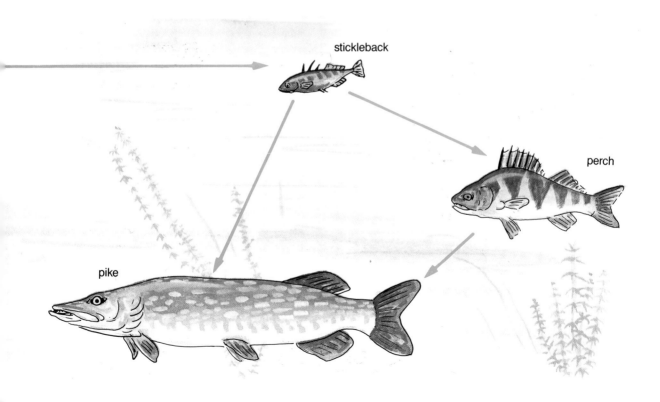

stickleback

perch

pike

11. A drink of water

In places where there are not too many people and very little industry, it is still possible to drink the water from a stream or a well. The water is cleaned as it runs over the stones and filters through the soil and can be drunk without any worry.

Towns and cities have too many people and too many factories in them to get their water from wells. They also need too much water. In the developing countries, each person needs about 12 litres of water a day. In the industrialized countries each person uses about 150 litres a day with half of this used in the home for drinking, cooking, washing and to flush the lavatory. The other half is used by industries.

Towns and cities take their water from lakes, rivers and from reservoirs. If it is possible, reservoirs are built high up in hills or mountains. They are filled by clean headstreams with few salts dissolved in them and very little life. That water will be easy to clean, or purify.

If this is not possible, and the reservoir is built near the lowland part of a river, then the water is stored for some time. This is so that the mud will naturally settle out and most dangerous disease-carrying bacteria will die.

Humans have not been able to invent anything that cleans water better than the plants and animals that do it naturally. Special tanks are built for them in water purification works. The water trickles through beds of sands with algae and bacteria in them. If the water has come downriver from another town, the water engineers may add chlorine or ozone, or radiate the water with ultraviolet light to make quite sure that any disease-carrying bacteria are dead. The water is then piped through the streets to the houses, so that you can turn a tap and have a drink of clean water.

The chain of reservoirs that provide some of the water for London.

Activity: Make a water filter

What you will need

A large plastic bottle, a plastic straw, some cotton wool, a clamp and two jars. You will also need some coarse gravel, fine gravel, large-grained sand, some fine sand and some absorbent paper.

Pierce a hole in the lid of the bottle large enough to fit the plastic straw. Put the straw through the lid. Cut the bottom from the bottle and clamp it upside down. Pack the neck of the bottle with cotton wool.

Then put in a layer of large gravel, then a layer of small gravel, then the large-grained sand followed by the fine sand and finally cover the top layer with the absorbent paper.

Pour muddy water into the top from one jar, collecting it in the other jar, placed under the straw. The water should be fairly clear when it drips out, but repeat the process if necessary. Try it with pond water and water with ink in it.

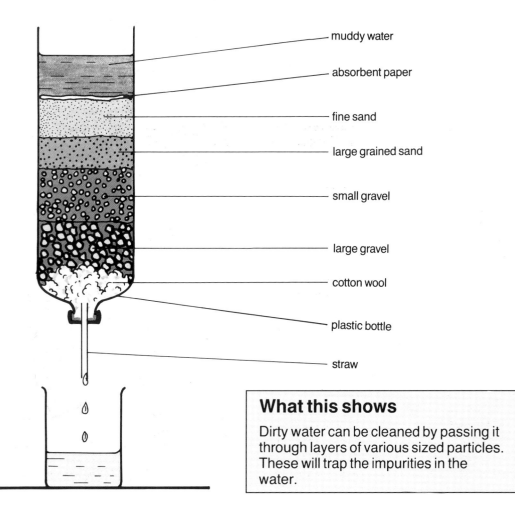

- muddy water
- absorbent paper
- fine sand
- large grained sand
- small gravel
- large gravel
- cotton wool
- plastic bottle
- straw

What this shows

Dirty water can be cleaned by passing it through layers of various sized particles. These will trap the impurities in the water.

12. Sewers and sewage

Places like towns and cities, where a great many people live together, produce another problem besides the need for a water supply. They produce a lot of waste from their bodies. These wastes may contain disease-carrying bacteria and they must be removed and cleaned as soon as possible. Wastes which are left can spread diseases like cholera.

Underground pipes, called sewers, do not only take wastes to the sewage works. They carry waste water from factories and rainwater too. Factories must not allow anything in their wastes that will damage the bacteria in the sewage works. These works are designed to give the algae and bacteria that feed on the wastes the best conditions to work in.

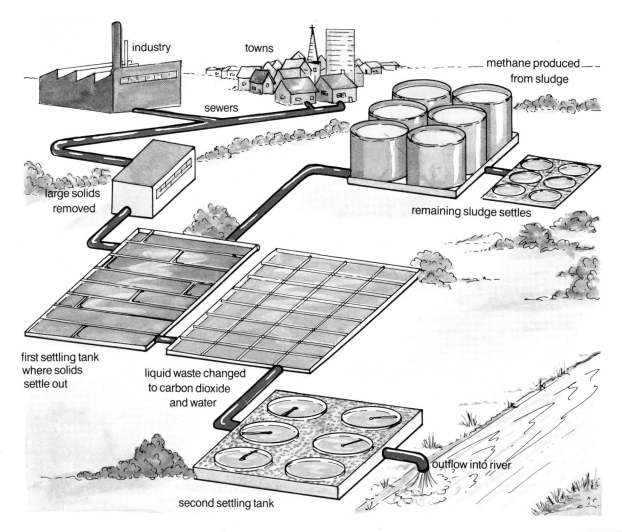

Waste from homes and factories is treated at modern sewage works. The solid waste is treated so it can be used in agriculture or dumped at sea. The liquid waste is treated so the water can be returned to the river.

Sewage engineers and scientists work in the sewage farms to make sure that the bacteria can clean all the waste from a town or part of a city.

The wastes are first taken through a grid which sieves out stones, gravel and large solids. The rest goes into a settling tank, where the floating particles sink to the bottom. The sludge from the bottom goes into airproof tanks where anaerobic bacteria feed on it. It is not reduced to carbon dioxide and water but to methane, which can be used as a power source. The liquids go into a tank with plenty of oxygen, where bacteria that need oxygen feed on it, changing the wastes to carbon dioxide and water. The water travels through another settling tank leaving clean water, which flows into the river or the sea.

In crowded parts of the world the water that leaves one town will be used again fairly quickly by a town further down the river. If it is for drinking it will need to be treated again.

An aerial view of a sewage works showing the settling tanks in the foreground.

The treated water from a sewage works rejoins the river.

13. Going to the sea

All the water eventually ends up in the seas, flowing out from a river or from melting snow or ice at the poles. Unfortunately not all the water returning to the seas will be clean. Factories do not always clean the water they return to the rivers. It may carry chemicals with it, and it may also carry heat. Heat pollution can change a river by raising the temperature so that the usual plants and animals cannot live in it.

Factories are not the only culprits. Farmers put pesticides on their land that are washed into streams where they can poison plants and animals as they are swept along. All this invisible pollution will be washed to the sea with solid rubbish, like plastics, that people throw into rivers.

Once it has reached the sea, the pollution can travel around the planet. The insecticide DDT, which cannot be decayed by bacteria, has been found in the bodies of penguins in the Antarctic. The insecticide must have travelled thousands of kilometres through the seas, and through the bodies of insects and fishes, from the place where it was first used, to be taken in by the penguins.

Not all the pollution in the seas comes down to rivers. Some is dumped straight into the sea by humans. Laws do not stop some oil tankers from cleaning out the oil left in their tanks and sending oil slicks that damage the sea birds and make beaches filthy.

Another problem is the dumping of waste from nuclear power stations into the sea. Radioactive wastes have been sealed in containers and dropped into deep ocean waters. If the wastes were to leak out they could enter the food chain. Some radioactive substances would be taken in by tiny marine creatures which would be eaten by small fish. Larger fish would then consume the small ones. The final link in the chain might be humans, eating the contaminated fish.

A beach polluted by sewage in South Australia.

Activity: Dispersing oil

What you will need

A glass bottle of water fitted with a stopper or cork, some lubicating oil and some household detergent.

Add two or three drops of oil to the water and watch what happens. Does the oil mix with the water?

Add a few drops of detergent and shake the bottle vigorously. Can you still see the oil?

Repeat with ten drops of oil, and then with twenty, counting the total number of drops of oil in the water. Do you reach a point when the water can no longer hold any more oil?

What thls shows

Oil can be dispersed with detergents. The oil does not disappear, but is broken up into tiny droplets and spreads through the water.

Rescuing cormorants which have been covered in oil following an oil spill at sea. The oil will have to be painstakingly removed from their feathers.

14. The sunlit seas

The sunlit top layer of the sea is very important. It is the biggest 'oxygen factory' on the planet, supplying a large part of the oxygen in the atmosphere. It is also the power plant of the oceans, the place where the Sun's energy is trapped by the plants and stored as food. The energy stored by the tiny floating plants, the phytoplankton, is used by all the living things on the surface, and down in the depths.

The sunlit top layer of the oceans is important because it is so large. It covers seven-tenths of the planet and goes down at least 100 m. Many millions of plants live in the phytoplankton which drifts in these layers, with many more plants, by weight, than those that live on land.

On the shores at the edges of the seas there are seaweeds, which are large, many-celled algae. Some of the large algae float in the surface waters. Sargasso weed is the most famous example of these. It collects in the Sargasso Sea in the North Atlantic and in other places.

A giant seaweed reaching up to the surface of the ocean off the Pacific coast. This particular type can reach up from depths of 40m and grow to a length of 60m.

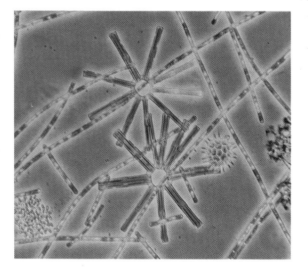

A close-up view of phytoplankton, the minute plants that drift in the upper layers of the oceans.

Animals do not have to stay in the surface layers, where the sunlight is, as the plants must do. They can swim down, but there are still some which spend most of their time in the surface waters. Floating animals like jellyfish, snails and worms stay on or near the surface. All the animals that drift instead of swimming are called plankton. The swimming animals are called nekton.

The concentration of the salt in the sea is extremely important to animals. If a solution of water and salt is separated by a material such as a fish's skin, the water will move from the weaker solution to the stronger one. Salt will move in the opposite direction. This process is called osmosis and sea animals have to balance the amount of salt in their bodies to prevent water loss.

Activity: To show osmosis

What you will need

A thin glass tube, some visking tubing, a beaker of salty water and some strong thread.

Tie one end of the visking tubing very firmly and fill it with water. Insert the tube and tie the other end tightly around it so that you have a 'balloon' of water with some water visible up the tube.

Place this in a beaker of very salty water which has been stirred so that most of the salt has dissolved. Mark the level of water in the tube and leave it for about an hour.

After this time check the level. What has happened? How can you explain this?

What this shows

Water has left the visking tubing and entered the strong salt solution by the process called osmosis. The visking tubing is rather like the skin of a fish and water tends to pass out of such a 'skin' into a stronger solution.

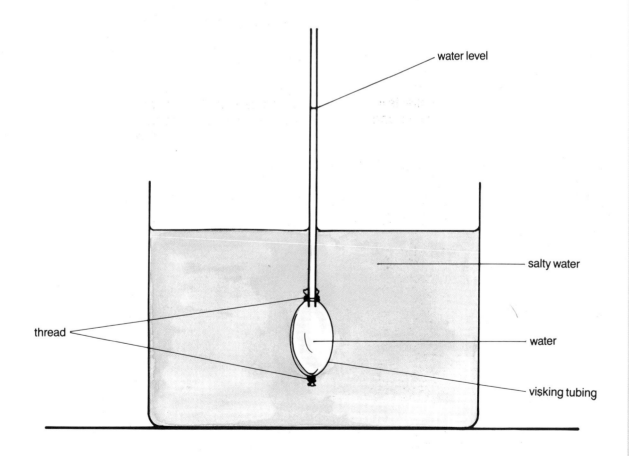

water level

salty water

thread

water

visking tubing

15. Life in the dark

By far the largest living space on the planet is dark and cold and under great pressure. At the bottom of the seas, the weight of all the hundreds of cubic metres of water presses down and no light can penetrate.

The animals that live in the deep waters feed on the detritus, the plant and animal remains that drift down from above, or live by hunting and eating other animals. The deep water hunting fishes have large jaws and long sharp teeth, so that they can swallow their prey even if it is very large. There are not as many living things in the depths as there would be in the surface waters and the hunters must search for their food.

The fishes can move up and down the waters by means of their air sacs. These balloon-like sacs inside their bodies can fill with gas to make the fish lighter, so that it will rise. The

Brightly coloured anthias swimming amongst corals in the Red Sea.

gas is emptied out of the sac to make the fish sink again. The fishes swim above the animals that live on the bottom. Corals, sponges, starfishes and prawns are all found feeding on the sea bed, sifting food out of the water and from the bottom mud.

These creatures do not live in a still, flat world. There are mountains and valleys on the sea bed, just as there are on land. The deepest valley, the Marianas Trench, is so deep that if Mount Everest, the world's highest mountain, were sunk in it, it would still be 2,000 m below the surface. Even at that depth prawns and brittle-stars are found.

The underwater landscape is swept by currents of cold water, sinking from the poles and moving across the beds, collecting mineral salts from the sea bed and the mud. There may be several currents flowing through the depths, going in different directions at different levels, occasionally rising to the surface, taking the nutrients with them.

Brittle-stars are often found at the bottom of the oceans.

Activity: Pressure and depth

What you will need

A large plastic bottle, some water, a water tank or bowl, some sticky tape and a ruler.

Cut off the top of the bottle and pierce five holes, in a straight line, in the remaining cylinder. Cover each hole with a piece of tape. Position the bottle on a stand above the tank and fill it with water.

Remove the top piece of tape and, with the ruler, measure how far the water travels away from the bottle. Replace the tape and refill the bottle with water. Now remove the second piece of tape and again measure the distance travelled away from the bottle.

Repeat this for all the remaining holes, refilling each time. What do you notice? What is the reason for this? Finally, remove all the pieces of tape and continually pour water into the bottle.

What this shows

The weight of water pressing down causes pressure. The pressure is greatest, causing the water to be pushed out with the greatest force, at the bottom of the bottle. This is because all the water is pressing down and pressure increases with depth.

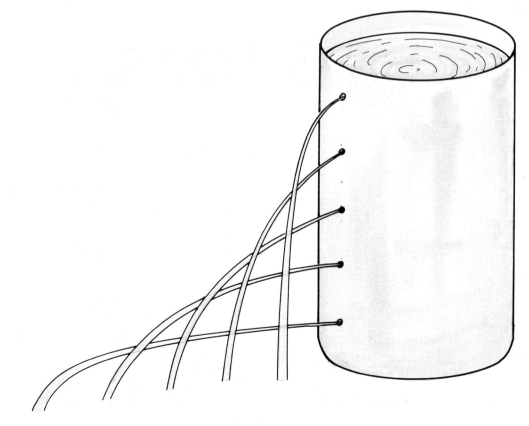

16. Plankton to people

The great stores of energy built up by the phytoplankton in the seas are tapped by humans when they go fishing. The plankton can certainly feed large quantities of animals. For instance tiny floating animals feed on the plankton and are in turn eaten by shoals of herring and cod. These in turn may be eaten by larger sea creatures or birds. The phytoplankton are at the start of such food chains and humans are often at the end of them.

Few species of fish are, in fact, of interest as food but as the world demand for food increases people are looking harder at fish from the seas. Recently many of the world's

Fish at a dockside market ready for transportation to the shops.

fishing industries have been catching fewer and fewer fish. The reason for this is that too many fish have been caught in the past and the ecology of the seas has been upset.

Until recently, there were no controls over the size of the mesh in fishing nets. If the mesh is large enough to catch adult fish but let the young escape, there will be a stock of adult fish for the next season. If the mesh is small, however, too many young fish will be taken and there will be a shortage. Many countries now have laws which make sure that the nets have a large enough mesh.

Bringing aboard a catch of herring from a trawler in the Atlantic.

New machinery like radar to seek out shoals, 'vacuum cleaner' machines to scoop up fish stocks and other sea animals and plants, and factory ships have added to the overfishing of the seas.

Food chains have also been affected. The overfishing of one species of fish has meant that there is more plankton for other species to take their place. Certain sea birds have also been affected as their natural food is taken by humans.

It is not just the fish numbers that are suffering. Marine mammals have also been severely hunted for food and products like oil. The whale population is shrinking so quickly that several species are near extinction. The big sea mammals breed very slowly and humans have been killing them faster than they can produce young to replace those that are lost. The Earth may lose the largest animal that has ever lived on the planet, the blue whale, because some countries are still ignoring the international laws made to protect it.

Although it is important to feed the people on the planet, we are in danger of killing off some of the creatures with which we share the Earth. Fish farming is now becoming an attractive way of producing some of our food requirements. This is where fish are reared from eggs in special farms and shellfish like oysters and mussels are already being grown in vast numbers.

The tail of a sperm whale strapped to the side of a whaling ship.

17. Harnessing the water

Humans have used water power for a long time. Some 2,000 years ago the Romans used water to drive mills for the grinding of corn. More recently water power has been used to produce electricity. Dams that are built to store water often have hydroelectric power stations built beneath them. Such power stations use the energy of fast-flowing water from a river or falling from a reservoir. The water turns the blades of a turbine which generates electricity.

The seas are another great store of energy. The power of the sea moves soil and rocks great distances and erodes the coastal

The French tidal power station at Rance. The motion of the advancing and retreating tides is used to produce electricity.

regions. The tides are caused by the pull of gravity of the Moon and the Sun and it is the winds that cause the powerful waves.

There have been many attempts to convert the rocking energy of the waves into electricity and countries which have a large area of coastline have been experimenting with different designs of wave energy converters.

Using the energy of the tides, however, may be more practical. One successful electricity station using tidal power is at Rance, on the northern coast of France. Here, the difference between high tide and low tide is very great and the blades of a turbine are turned when the tide comes in or goes out.

A further method of extracting energy from the seas has been suggested. This takes advantage of the fact that the surface regions of the oceans trap a lot of heat. The idea is to use this heat to convert a liquid with a low boiling point, like ammonia, into a gas. The gas would expand and drive a turbine in an undersea power station to create electricity. The gas would then be pumped in pipes down to the colder layers of the ocean so it would turn back to a liquid for pumping back to the surface to start the cycle again.

An old water wheel that was used in the industrial revolution.

Activity: Make a water wheel

What you will need

Three corks, a plastic bottle, a metal knitting needle and some thread.

Cut four slits in the cork, each at right angles to one another and carefully push the needle through the centre of the cork and then remove it. Cut a square from one side of the bottle and cut this up into four equal sized strips the same length as the cork. Push these strips into the slits in the cork so you have a 'wheel'.

Make two holes in the bottle above the square hole and place the wheel through the hole. Push the needle through the holes and cork so that it spins easily. Then push the other corks onto each end of the needle.

Now tie a length of thread to one of the exposed ends of the needle and to the other end of the thread tie a small weight, like a pencil. Cut a hole in the bottom of the bottle and hold it upside down under a tap. Run water into the bottle. What do you see? What happens when you turn the tap on more?

What this shows

Water can be used to turn a wheel which can do some work. For example, it could power a turbine to generate electricity.

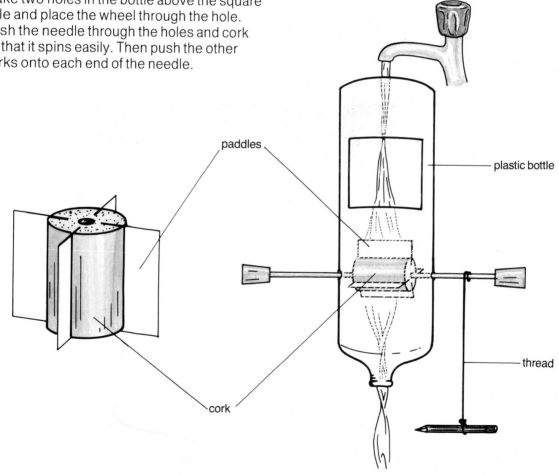

paddles

plastic bottle

cork

thread

18. What can we do?

Humans are already beginning to do something about the pollution of the planet's waters and there have been many successes. One of the biggest success stories is the cleaning up of the river Thames in the UK. A century ago, the Thames was little more than an open sewer. There were many towns and cities along the length of the river, each pouring untreated sewage into it.

With these wastes and the material from new factories the bacteria in the Thames could not cope and the river almost died. Very few plants and animals could survive in it and there was a very real danger of humans catching fatal diseases from it. The Victorians began the cleaning process, building a network of sewers and sewage works. From 1900 onwards the river began to improve. Laws were made to stop factories putting poisonous wastes into the river and gradually fish began to return. By the 1980s the river was back to normal and salmon were seen, fish that are very sensitive to pollution.

In the USA some $50 billion has been spent in recent years, in an effort to stop the flow of raw sewage and industrial wastes into the nation's waterways. Successful laws have reduced the water pollution by over one-third. However, there are still a great many problems. The burial of poisonous chemicals has contaminated the water table in very many areas and the use of a single pesticide has meant that 1,400 wells in California's Central Valley have had to be closed.

On a smaller scale, people have been clearing up the fresh waters near them. Volunteers clean away the rubbish that has

Should the oxygen level in the Thames fall dangerously low, oxygen can be injected directly into the water at the scene of the problem.

Taking a sample of water from the sea for pollution testing.

been dumped in rivers, lakes and ponds, and can dispose of the plastic materials before they are washed into the sea.

All the improvements to fresh water help to reduce the pollution of the seas. Environmental groups have drawn the attention of the world to major issues such as the dumping of nuclear waste in the oceans and the discharge of such waste into the sea. Their campaigns have persuaded many governments to stop the dumping of wastes and to gradually reduce the amount discharged.

Similar campaigns have been successful in banning the hunting of whales. An international agreement was made to stop this but Japan, Russia and Norway have refused to abide by this decision. It is up to the people of these, and other nations to encourage their governments to stop the over-exploitation of the seas and to reduce the pollution of our planet's water.

Pressure groups like Greenpeace have done much to persuade governments to reduce the amount of wastes dumped into the sea.

Glossary

Absorption The taking in of a substance.

Acid rain Rain is normally slightly acid. Yet gases like the oxides of sulphur and nitrogen, which are released into the air by burning fuels like coal, dissolve in the water in the air and fall as acid rain, snow or mist.

Algae A major group of plants of very simple form. They contain chlorophyll but lack proper stems, roots and leaves.

Anaerobic Not needing oxygen or air.

Aquifer A rock, such as sandstone, that can absorb water and can be used to supply wells.

Atmosphere The layer of gases that surround a planet, held there by gravity.

Bacteria Extremely small living things which bring about the decay of plant and animal remains and wastes.

Capillarity The process where liquids naturally rise through the tiny spaces between solids.

Carbon dioxide A colourless gas that makes up 0.03 per cent of the air. It is released through the respiration of living things.

Catchment area The area of land which drains water into a river or lake.

Cell All living things are made up of cells, the smallest units of life.

Chlorophyll The green chemical in plants that absorbs the light energy required for photosynthesis.

Cholera A severe illness caused by taking in unclean water or food.

Convection A process by which heat travels through air or a liquid.

DDT A colourless substance used to control insect pests on crops. It is poisonous to animals and builds up in the body.

Decay To rot as a result of the action of bacteria or fungi.

Energy The power to do work.

Environment The world around us, or our surroundings, including all living things. The place where an animal or plant lives may be called its environment.

Estuary The widening channel of a river where it nears the sea, with a mixing of freshwater and sea water.

Evaporation The change of a liquid into a vapour.

Fertilizer Any substance, such as manure, added to soil to increase its productivity.

Food chain A chain of living things through which energy is passed as food.

Fresh water Water that is free of salt dissolved in it. This makes up only three per cent of the world's water.

Gulf stream A warm ocean current flowing northeastwards off the Atlantic coast of the USA from the Gulf of Mexico.

Headstream A stream that is the source or a source of a river.

Hibernate To go into a deep sleep over the cold winter months.

Hydroelectric power Energy that is generated from falling water. It is often shortened to HEP.

Ice ages Periods in the Earth's history when ice has covered a large part of its surface.

Larva(e) The grub that hatches from an insect's egg.

Marine To do with the seas and oceans.

Methane A gas given off by decaying plant and animal remains as they are eaten by bacteria.

Minerals Substances which occur naturally in the Earth.

Nekton The swimming animals that live in the middle-depths of a sea or lake.

Nitrogen The gas that makes up 78 per cent of the atmosphere.

Osmosis The process in which a solvent passes from a weak solution into a stronger one through a substance like a fishes skin.

Oxygen The gas that makes up nearly 21 per cent of the atmosphere. It is essential for life.

Ozone A gas that is a form of oxygen. A layer of this gas exists in the atmosphere.

Pesticide A chemical used for killing pests like insects and rodents.

pH scale The scale that measures how acid or alkaline a substance is. Pure water has a pH of seven. Acids have a pH of less than this and alkalis have a higher pH.

Photosynthesis The food-making process carried out by green plants. The Sun's energy is absorbed by chlorophyll in plants to make food from carbon dioxide and water.

Phytoplankton The tiny green plants that float in water.

Plankton The small drifting plants and animals that live in the surface layer of a sea or lake.

Pollution The release of substances into the air, water or land that may upset the natural balance of the environment. Such substances are called pollutants.

Radioactive Something that gives out harmful rays.

Residue The material remaining after something has been removed.

Sap A solution of mineral salts and sugars that flows in a plant.

Sewage A mixture of water and waste products from homes or industry that is carried away in underground pipes called sewers.

Solvent A substance, usually a liquid, which dissolves other substances in it.

Thermocline A boundary in a lake or pond where above it is warm water and below it is cold water.

Ultraviolet rays A dangerous form of energy which is deadly to most life.

Water cycle The circulation of the Earth's water, in which water evaporates from the sea into the atmosphere where it turns back to a liquid and falls as rain or snow. The water returns to the sea in rivers or evaporates again.

Water table The surface of the water which is held in the ground.

Water vapour Water in the form of a gas.

Further information

Books to read

Barret, H. **Focus on Seafood** (Wayland, 1986)

Bently, J. & Charlston, B. **Finding Out About Streams** (Batsford, 1985)

Carson, R. **Silent Spring** (Penguin, 1982)

Central Electricity Generating Board **Acid Rain** (CEGB, 1984)

Clegg, J. **Freshwater Life** (Frederick Warne, 1974)

Cochrane, J. **Exploring Ecology** (Macdonald Educational, 1974)

Corliss, M. **Focus on Water** (Wayland, 1985)

Dyson, J. **The Pond Book** (Puffin, 1976)

Earth Resources Research **The Acid Rain Controversy** (ERR, 1984)

Elsworth, S. **Acid Rain** (Pluto Press, 1984)

Hilary, E. **Ecology 2000** (Michael Joseph, 1984)

Leutscher, A. **The Ecology of Water Life** (Franklin Watts, 1971)

Linley, M. **Discovering Frogs and Toads** (Wayland, 1986)

Rowland-Entwistle, T. **Rivers and Lakes** (Wayland, 1986)

Thompson, G., Coldrey, J. & Bernard, G. **The Pond** (Collins, 1984)

Whitton, B. **Rivers, Lakes and Marshes** (Hodder & Stoughton, 1979)

Williams, D.I. & Anglesea, D. **Experiments on Water Pollution** (Wayland, 1978)

Young, G. **Pollution** (Edward Arnold, 1980)

Organizations to contact

Australian Conservation Foundation,
672b Glenferrie Road,
Hawthorn,
Victoria 3122

Council for Environmental Education,
London Ecology Centre,
45 Shelton Street,
London WC2H 9HJ
UK

**Environment and Conservation
Organizations of New Zealand Inc. (ECO),**
PO Box 11057,
Wellington,
NZ

Friends of the Earth (UK),
377 City Road,
London EC1V 1NA

Greenpeace (Canada),
427 Bloor Street West,
Toronto,
Ontario

Greenpeace (UK),
36 Graham Street,
London N1 2JX

National Trust,
36 Queen Anne's Gate,
London SW1H 9AS
UK

National Wildlife Federation,
1412 16th Street NW,
Washington DC 20036,
USA

Royal Society for Nature Conservation,
22 The Green,
Nettleham,
Lincoln LN2 2NR,
UK

British Trust for Conservation Volunteers,
36 St Mary's Street,
Wallingford,
Oxon. OX10 0EU

Earthscan,
3 Endsleigh Street,
London WC1 0DD
UK

Friends of the Earth (Australia),
National Liaison Office,
366 Smith Street,
Collingwood,
Victoria 3065

Friends of the Earth (USA),
530 7th Street SE,
Washington DC 20003

Greenpeace (New Zealand),
Private Bag,
Wellesley Street,
Auckland

National Campaign Against Toxic Hazards,
2000 P Street NW,
Washington DC 20009,
USA

Young National Trust,
PO Box 12,
Westbury,
Wilts. BA13 4NA
UK

Pollution Probe,
12 Madison Avenue,
Ontario M5R 2S1,
Canada

Thames Water,
Public Relations Department,
New River Head,
Rosebery Avenue,
London EC1R 4TP,
UK

Index

Picture acknowledgements

The author and the publishers would like to thank the following for allowing their illustrations to be reproduced in this book: Ardea, 18, David Bowden 21 (bottom); Bruce Coleman Limited cover (bottom J. Foott, left K. Taylor), frontispiece (NASA), 16 (C. Bonington), 20 (K. Taylor), 21 (H. Reinhard), 22 (R. Wilmshurst), 26 (E. Crichton), 31 (M.W. Richards/RSPB), 32 top (F. Sauer), bottom (J. Foott), 36 (W. Ferchland), 37 (G. Williamson), 38 (C. Molyneux); Cecilia Fitzsimons 8, 9, 11, 13, 14, 17, 19, 23, 24–25, 27, 28, 33, 35, 39; G.S.F. Picture Library cover (right R.J. Teede), 30; Greenpeace 41; Hutchison Library 12; Thames Water 29 (both), 40 (bottom); Zefa Picture Library 6 (Halin), 7, 34 (both), 38 (bottom). All other illustrations from Wayland Picture Library.